My Way to
OUR WAY™

My Way to OUR WAY™

Win-Win training for <u>any</u> situation.

Jessie Upp, M.S.

Epoch Media
Seattle, Washington

My Way to Our Way™ - Reinvent Your Life
Copyright © 2007 by Jessie Upp
Cover by Lulu
Internal Design by Jessie Upp
Edited by Karin Bigelow

This publication is designed to provide authoritative information in regard to the subject matter covered. It is sold with the understanding that the publisher is not engaged in rendering legal, accounting, or other professional service. If legal advice or other expert assistance is required, the services of a competent or professional person should be sought. – *From A Declaration of Principles Jointed Adopted by a Committee of the American Bar Association and a Committee of Publishers and Associations.*

All brand names and product names used in this book are trademarks of their respective holders. Epoch Media is not associated with any product or vendor in this book. Epoch Media books may be purchased for educational or business use.

FIRST EDITION

All inquires should be addressed to:
Epoch Media
PO Box 84
Marblemount, WA 98026

Library of Congress Cataloging-in-Publication Data is available upon request.

International Standard Book No.: 978-0-6151-5980-5

Printed and bound in the United States of America.
10 9 8 7 6 5 4 3 2 1

To all the people out there
who want to be part of the solution,
rather than the problem.

www.myway2ourway.com

Contents

"When I realize someone else's solution
has become MY problem,
I either can choose to be a part of the problem
or part of the solution."

This Activity Book
belongs to:

_____

Month/YEAR:

_____

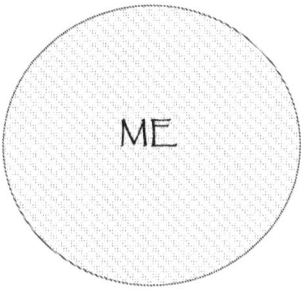

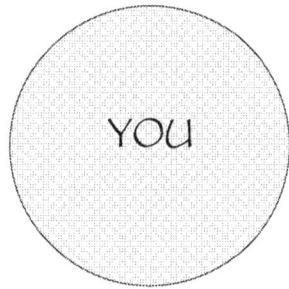

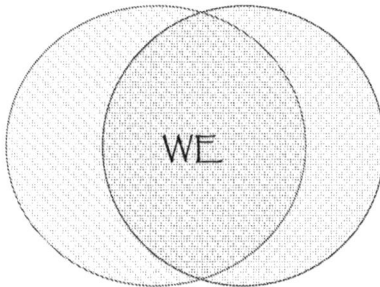

Introduction

The world is a place for contribution and constant creation.

Over the first third of my life, I looked at the world and myself as something to improve. Though that gave me meaning, I never felt like I was fully appreciating each moment. I found out I'm not the only one, so I set out to out to view the world differently.

I came to see that my idea of improvement sometimes turned into someone else's problem. I didn't want to be a part of the problem, so I chose to create a way to be a part of the entire solution, a way that requires seeing infinite possibilities. Infinite possibilities result from tapping into all that we are. Some refer to this as serving internal motivation, God, the Source, etc. In this curriculum, I refer to this as serving our *Purpose*.

The basic aim of this book is for all participants to relate to Life as simply a _possibility_ to create peaceful interactions, loving moments, safety, & a sense of belonging – NOT struggle, limitation & something to overcome. I produced this book to share the process of transforming My Way to OUR WAY™ with you.

My Way to OUR WAY™ is an interactive training workbook that provides a life method used to live life values and relationship promises. This short and sweet, visually intensive book includes _fifteen activities and an action plan._

How to Use This Activity Book

You might have grown up learning that you <u>are</u> your age, your feelings, and your possessions. You might even believe that others have the power to <u>make</u> you angry and didn't learn that you are solely responsible for your own happiness. You didn't make these beliefs consciously. Countless messages of inadequacy are woven into your every day life. As you move through this book, you will start to build your life the way it was intended.

You will begin this book by examining your language and the huge effect it has on limiting how you see the world, either as limited or limitless. These activities are meant to be completed in **chronological order**, as the exploration of your identity addresses the following activities of behavior and the power of choice.

Integrate each activity into your daily life. You will see your language transform from "I can't" or "I'll try" **into a life of** "I will" and "I choose to."

As a paradigm shifter, this tool will not only provide insight, but will reframe life and the events that unfold. I know it will give you the necessary means to reinvent your life so that you not only ARE great, but <u>feel</u> great.

Have fun! ☺

Jessie Upp

Part One: It's All About ME!
[My Way] to Our Way

Language

The very thought of language can be overwhelming. Without analyzing our language, it is difficult to reframe the way we see life and people around us, even the way we see ourselves.

Because your language is a result of your beliefs, you now get to explore your beliefs backwards! In every phrase you state, in every response you give, in every reaction you choose, you have words and non-verbal communication. Both are essential to communicating to others. Both highlight the sort of game you are playing in life.

Without knowing how you speak, you may not know how you think. If you don't know how you think, you are simply <u>reacting</u> to life rather than <u>creating</u>.

Let's break it down now. Find the way you build your life by the words you choose. Words are very powerful, for they act as a model of your world.

We are responsible for the life we invent.

Activity 1: The Missing Word

It is important to see how every descriptive word in the English sentence is missing a very important word: BEING. We have invented this language and it has determined how we see the world. You've grown up with right/wrong, bad/good, and beautiful/ugly.

Write the word "being" after the word "are" or "is" in the sentences below:

1.   I'm glad you are _____ my team-mate.
2.   You are _____ funny!
3.   You always are _____ happy.
4.   He always is _____ a great player.
5.   She is not _____ fair.

Start to place this delicate word in every descriptive word you say about yourself or another person. Know the description is simply temporary - because it is not always happening. Now, you try! Fill in the blanks below.

_____ is <u>BEING</u> _____.

- Are we what we DO?
  Sometimes we are doing that. Sometimes we aren't.
- Are we what we FEEL?
  Sometimes we are feeling that. Sometimes not.
- Are we what we HAVE?
  Sometimes we have that. Sometimes we don't.
- Are we what we ACHIEVE?
  Sometimes we achieve. Sometimes not.

You now see the power in the words we choose. Once you add that little powerful word to all that you think, it affects all that you say. What you say affects the people in your life. Can you see that the adjectives you speak are <u>missing</u> this powerful little word?

You see, someone can describe themselves as a **parent** and they will be identified as a parent, but you can look beyond this as an identifier to their life and see it as an identifier to their moments. If a parent is not a child, but they are acting as a **child**, are they really 'being' a parent in that moment? Not in this curriculum.

Please note that you can spend your energy debating this as true or untrue, but we are simply inventing something here – something that works for your life in a way that you have not yet imagined or experienced. Please continue on as if this is a game that you are learning, and the Rules are being explained to you as you play!

Self-Imposed Rules

Now that you know that the language you have learned has actually limited the world you live in, take a few minutes to ponder how language confines expression.

What if you were told that your internal language (thoughts) determines your problems? What if you were told that your problems were simply someone else's solutions?

Read on to find out more...

Activity 2: My Current Thoughts & Behaviors
(These activities were designed to be completed in chronological order)

How do you think, feel and play in life?

The statements below determine the life you've been living - up until now. If you agree to the statement on the left, write YES in right column. If you don't agree, write NO. If you answer YES to the final statement (#10), you are ready to begin! After completing this book, you might want to come back here and see if any of your "belief" statements change.

1.	I believe that <u>every</u>thing said (internally and externally) has a positive intention.	
2.	I believe positive intentions can be found in both constructive and destructive behaviors.	
3.	I only have positive thoughts and feelings about myself and others.	
4.	I believe that I am the cause of my own feelings.	
5.	I don't blame my negative or positive feelings/behaviors on others. For example: "You make me so mad!" or "You made me do it!" or "You make me so happy!"	
6.	I want to enjoy life, regardless if I win or lose.	
7.	I want others to see me as enjoying life, regardless of whether or not I am successful.	
8.	I am willing to contribute to the lives of others.	
9.	I want others to feel peaceful, loving and safe around me.	
10.	I am <u>willing</u> to reinvent my life so that all the statements above can be answered with a YES.	

Activity 3: My Rules!

Think about some personal responsibilities you think EVERYONE should have in life. For example, you may say people should not yell at others in anger.

Write 3 of these Rules down here.

1)

2)

3)

Has someone broken one of these Rules lately?
Who was it?

1. Rules are internal truths, but can be agreed upon.
2. Each of the above statements is a rule you have created to win at your own game.
3. These Rules are justified, but are not ultimate truths, because Rules can be argued. You may say someone broke your Rule, but you may have broken theirs, too.
4. Your Rules aren't right/wrong, but you may have invented this.
5. These Rules are not who you are.

17

Activity 4: Broken Rules

Next time you are upset at someone, consider that your rule simply didn't meet <u>their</u> needs. In the left circle below, write a rule you wrote in Activity 3 that was recently broken. Write the person's name in the right circle.

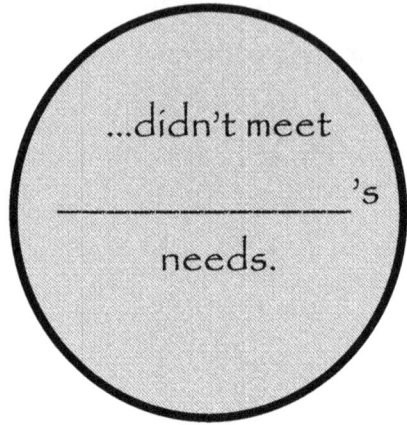

My Rule...

...didn't meet

_____'s

needs.

How did your Rule limit you?
How did your Rule limit them?
You will only be satisfied until your next Rule is broken... Broken Rules make problems. Why do <u>you</u> live by Rules?

18

Behavior

Again, when we are being upset with someone, it feels as if we are on the "losing" team...even though we are on the same team (called Life). This is because you both never took the time to agree on the original Rules!

Your Rules only meet your needs and not the needs of others. Their Rules only meet their needs and not yours. Sometimes this works, but sooner or later, Rules clash. What makes you right makes another wrong. What might make you confident might make another uneasy. What makes you win makes another lose. You may even struggle internally with this.

Now you are aware of the life game & Rules you have been playing so far. When you're upset, consider it as a gift telling you that you are playing this old game. Ever wonder why they say "Rules were meant to be broken"? It's because they are yours and they only meet your needs.

Do you really want to play a game of success - where it opens room for your own failure? Do you really want to play a game where your satisfaction only lives until someone breaks the next Rule of yours?

Of course not!

Read on to see where some of your Rules show up in your life...

Activity 5: My Advice, Requests, Habits

Please note your responses below.

A recent request I made, but went unmet:

Recent advice or suggestion I gave:

Your unmet requests, advice and suggestions (a.k.a Rules) were <u>more</u> <u>likely</u> made to meet your needs - rather than theirs.

A habit or addiction I have that I know is unhealthy:

Your habits are Rules made to <u>temporarily</u> give you a feeling of peace.

Recent advice I gave, but I don't always model:

Hypocrisy is a Rule you want others to follow, but won't follow yourself. This is because if THEY follow it, it meets your own needs and if YOU follow it, it does not meet your needs.

As you see, Rules work for you, but they may or may not work for others. You come up with certain solutions and you change them when they don't work. The more you feel like solutions don't work, the more your solutions may become destructive. This might include becoming upset, demanding someone to do something, or yelling.

20

Activity 6: No, Don't, Stop!

Rules that STOP someone from doing something don't invite what to START. Here, learn the power of turning a NO into a YES.

Try describing to someone how to NOT play a game of basketball. Remember, you can't tell them what to do, but <u>not</u> do! It's difficult isn't it?

Choose to turn your "NO!" Rules into "YES" Rules.
[No! Don't! and Stop!] do not offer any room for choice. If you demand that someone has NO choice in the matter, what type of relationship are you setting up?

Below, two different No! Rules pop up in one conversation, but both people share the same need & result: peace. They just have different solutions to "get to" peace. Notice that both No! Rules were turned into a Yes! Rule, but they still don't meet the needs of both people. This is still living by rules and "MY WAY," yet it is going to help you enter into the OUR WAY process...

Who?	NO! Rule	Yes Rule!	Need
YOU	Don't put your stinky feet on the couch!	I want your feet off the couch.	Peace
THEM	Don't yell at me!	I want my feet on the couch.	Peace

Now, you try. Below, turn the No! Rule into a Yes! Rule:

++

Who?	NO! Rule	Yes Rule!	Need
YOU	Stop whining!		Peace
THEM	Don't tell me what to do!		Peace

Write down your No! Rule and transform it below:

Who?	NO! Rule	Yes Rule!	Need
YOU			
THEM			

Activity 7: My Solutions

When you are faced with someone who is angry with you, who are you most likely to be? Write down the letters of your chosen solutions (strategies) in the two boxes below.

A.   Most of the time, I think about how the other person is wrong, but I won't say it to them. I keep it inside, walk away in a HUFF, or I go and share it with someone else.

B.   Most of the time, I think about what I did wrong and feel TERRIBLE that they are mad at me. I apologize, and try to make it better for them.

C.   Most of the time, I get ANGRY that they didn't think of my needs and I tell them that I won't be bullied!

D.   Most of the time, I have no idea where their anger came from. I get confused and don't know what to do.

When I react to someone else's anger,
or am frustrated at someone, most of the time
I will choose this Solution:

If that <u>doesn't work</u>, then most of the time
I will choose this Solution:

Activity 8: My Islands
When you do THAT, I do THIS...

See pg 42 for examples of the following behaviors.

When someone is doing something that annoys, frustrates, or even angers you, what do you do to get them to stop? How do you deal with conflict? How many islands (a.k.a. behaviors/solutions) can you think of? Shade in as many as you have used.

My Way:
(My Islands/Behaviors)

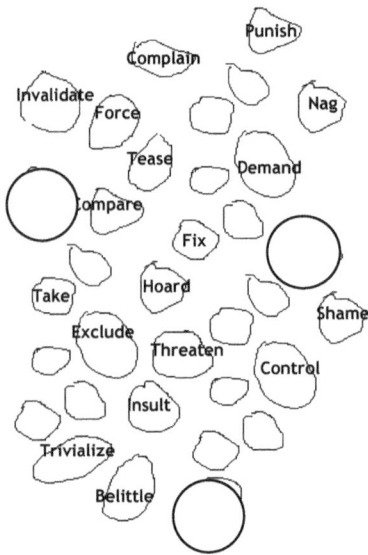

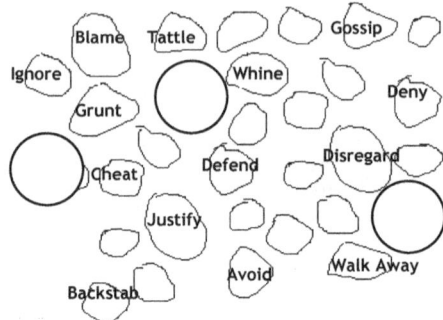

Blame Tattle Gossip
Ignore Whine
Grunt Deny
Cheat Defend Disregard
Justify
Backstab Avoid Walk Away

Punish
Complain
Invalidate Nag
Force
Tease Demand
Compare
Fix
Take Hoard
Shame
Exclude Threaten
Control
Insult
Trivialize
Belittle

Did you shade most of your islands in the top right? Then you probably chose "A" or "B" in Activity 7. These behaviors are the indirect solutions that hold in, hide, deflect, or substitute. If you apply these types of conflict styles, you often express your needs passively. You often put others first and might become bitter. If you become angry, you tend to express your frustrations with someone who is safe. In fact, you might RE press needs so much in life, you might get DE pressed. If depressed, you may get involved in over-eating, drugs, alcohol, or smoking so that you can temporarily feel your needs are being met.

Did you shade most of your islands in the bottom left? Then you probably chose "C" in Activity 7. These aggressive behaviors are very direct and out in the open. By using these conflict styles, you often approach others in which you are annoyed with and express your needs. These types of solutions don't create & maintain healthy relationships. If you choose these solutions as a way of dealing with others in the moment, it's highly likely that you will push these people out of your future.

Identity

Your identity is made up of many chosen expressions. You choose to express yourself in many ways, but the purpose underlying these expressions is always positive. These are referred to as Positive Intentions and they start to explore your Purpose, but are not always purposeful living. Your "Purpose" will be further explored in Activity 11.

Activity 9: My Positive Intention

In Column 2, write down some of the behaviors you shaded on Activity 8 and place it directly across from the positive intention YOU think is at the base of each of your behaviors. These behaviors are solutions you use to express your needs – but only after your failed positive solutions failed. Column 3 is how others might relate to your destructive solutions. You may feel the same feelings as well! At this point, your solution becomes their problem. Fill in Column 3 as you see appropriate.

COLUMN 1 Positive Intentions	COLUMN 2 If I've expressed my needs in constructive ways and they didn't work, I might EXPRESS my need in this destructive way:	COLUMN 3 This is how I might feel and others might feel - as a result of my chosen expression:
Peace	Example: I yell	Example: Aggravated
Safety		
Belonging		
Love		

Activity 10: Who Am I?

Trace your hand in the middle of the paper.
Ask yourself the question above.
What comes to mind?
Write your words <u>inside</u> your 3 fingers.
In the 4th finger, write "team-player."
Keep your thumb blank!

Activity 11: Is That Really Me?

Going back to Activity #1 (pg 14), please do the following:

1. Put the word "being" in front of anything you wrote that is not <u>constantly</u> happening.
   You are not ALWAYS happy.

2. Put "being" in front of anything you wrote that can change by force, or by nature.
   You are not ALWAYS 27 years old.

3. Put "being" in front of anything you wrote that is not <u>always</u> available to you.
   You are NOT your car.

4. Put "being" in front of anything you wrote that can be compared, as that comparison separates you from ALL others. Once you separate yourself, you do not fully belong. You live for the sense of belonging and the minute you compare, you are setting yourself up for a failed sense of belonging. This will <u>limit</u> your life and this curriculum is about <u>expanding</u> your life.

To BE and live on Purpose!

This curriculum is simply an invention and tool to express your Purpose:
Four ultimate identifiers for who you already are:

Peace, Safety, Belonging and Love.

Peace: To BE without anxiety (or fear) of the past or future. In the truest of expression, it is positively serving the moment:
as it is and not as it should or shouldn't be.

Safety: To BE without danger. In the truest of expression, it is positively serving your own mental and physical state.

Belonging: To BE without longing. In the truest of expression, it is positively connecting with something larger than you. For example: relationships, groups, or God.

Love: To BE without fear. In the truest of expression, it is positively serving your own needs so that the illusion of fear doesn't threaten your ability to contribute to yourself or others (your Purpose).

Your positive intention is to feel each of these. Your Purpose is NOT to feel them, but to actually choose them as your expressions - in all that you say and do. This is contributing with Purpose, or living on Purpose. In being peaceful, you feel peaceful. In being loving, you feel loving, etc. Lacking the contribution of any one of these sacrifices all four. They are all interconnected.

Activity 12: What Is MY Purpose?

When you were a baby, you were already every word in <u>Column 'A'</u>.
You can't debate it, it never changes, and it is always available to you!
You <u>live</u> to express these. This is your Purpose.

COLUMN A I was BORN with:	COLUMN B This is how I might EXPRESS this area of my Purpose in every day life:	COLUMN C This is how I might feel as a result of my chosen expression:
Peace	Example: I drink tea.	Example: Relaxed
Safety		
Belonging		
Love		

Now, go back to Activity 10 (pg 26). Look at each word you wrote in your fingers.

Before each word, add the little powerful word "being" <u>before</u> each of your identifiers. For example, if you wrote "funny," you would now read it as "being funny".

For each one, ask yourself, "Why do I choose to BE that?"

Why do you choose THAT form of expression?
What is it that you intend to feel as a result of being this?

Playing the game as if there are only <u>four</u> answers you can choose from, write down one of the following: peace, love, safety or belonging below each finger (and within the palm of your hand). You might find yourself writing the same answer for all four fingers! It will reveal your motivations.

In your thumb, write "CONTRIBUTE" in your most creative way.

In this curriculum, you live for creating and contributing so that you can experience your Purpose. When you create with another and contribute to another, you are suspending the desire to meet only your own ego (your own needs – MY WAY) and meeting the needs of all involved (OUR WAY).

As you move on through this curriculum, you will gain the tool to create and contribute – even in your most heated moments.

Part Two: It's All About YOU!
[My Way] to Our Way

The following activities will help illustrate how every act has a positive intention, regardless of any negative aspects. This positive intention is their objective to feel good. Learn to see through the eyes of another.

In Activity 13, "Islands" are used to describe various destructive behaviors. Some are aggressive and some are passive-aggressive. Passive-aggressive, in this context, means expressing your needs in a concealed manner that threatens another's needs. The following table includes a partial list of destructive behaviors (a.k.a. Solutions).

ISLAND or "DESTRUCTIVE SOLUTION"	DEFINTION	EXAMPLE
1. *%$#!	To express vulgar language, usually with a louder, declarative voice.	*%$#!
2. Avoid	To not approach the person I have a problem with. To come up with a way to NOT think about the problem I came up with.	[Staying clear of someone you don't want to talk to OR using some sort of escape as over-eating, drinking, smoking]
3. Backstab	To express fault or weakness in someone. To devalue a person that is not present.	"She can be so mean!"
4. Belittle	To regard as small importance and brush aside.	"Well, that doesn't really matter…"

5. Blame	To put responsibility on someone else for my feelings, choice, or actions. To point the finger at another.	*"She made me do it."*
6. Brag	To talk proudly about what I own or what I can do to impress another.	*"I have two of those!"*
7. Centralize	To talk a lot about myself, my ideas and my experiences. To interrupt and relate to what others say to something about me.	*"Oh! That reminds me of when I…"*
8. Cheat	To act dishonestly to get what I want.	*[Using any form of lying to get your way]*
9. Compare	To notice a difference between two people, or things. For example, what is available and not available.	*"If you were more like Jill, you'd be…"*
10. Complain	To express what I don't want, usually to a safe person.	*"I can't believe she would even do that!!"*
11. Confuse	To create a state of misunderstanding, either as the communicator, or the receiver. To attempt to make someone confused to appear right.	*"Well, you said Saturday and then Friday and I thought you mean next Friday!"*
12. Control	To use power when no control is being experienced. To have power over what will be and, more importantly, how it will be.	*"I need you to do this. No questions asked."*

A FULL list of destructive solutions is found in the Island Index (page 42).

Activity 13: Their Islands
THAT really disturbs me...

Think about certain behaviors that really annoy you, frustrate you, or even <u>anger</u> you. When you are with your friends, family, or co-workers, think about what <u>they</u> might do that really disturbs you. How many islands (a.k.a. behaviors/ solutions) can you think of? Shade in observed islands that annoy you most:

My Way:
(Their Behaviors/Solutions)

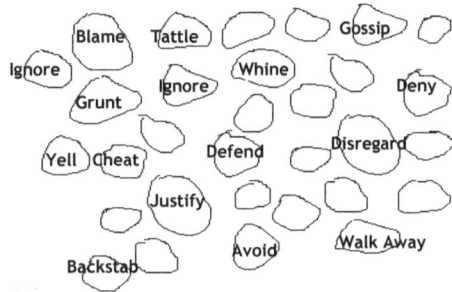

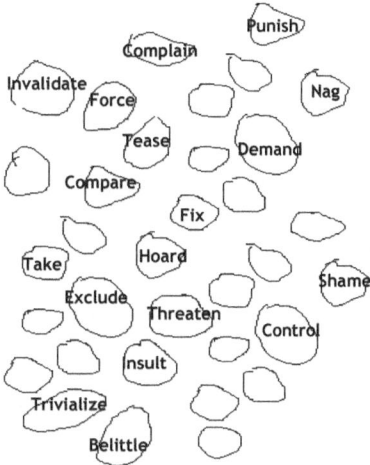

Blame Tattle Gossip
Ignore Whine Deny
Grunt Ignore
Yell Cheat Defend Disregard
Justify
Backstab Avoid Walk Away

Punish
Complain
Invalidate Nag
Force
Tease Demand
Compare
Fix
Take Hoard Shame
Exclude Threaten
Insult Control
Trivialize
Belittle

Below, write down three islands/solutions you shaded and jot down how you <u>feel</u> when it happens.

For example, when someone avoids me, I feel lonely.

<u>Behavior</u>		<u>Feeling</u>
Avoid	=	Lonely
_____		_____
_____		_____
_____		_____

(See Island Index for examples of destructive behaviors.)

Activity 14: Their Positive Intention

TIP OF THE ISLAND

Think of an <u>issue</u> you had with someone where you were upset. Write this down at the tip. Think of this as the tip of their Island and you are going to dive to find out their good intention.

Island Example: **Disregard**

What was their Island?

Issue Example: **They put their feet on the couch after saying they wouldn't.**

What is OBVIOUS:

ISSUE:

What is HIDDEN:

HELP

What do you think they <u>wanted</u>?

Example: **I think they just wanted to push my buttons.**

<u>Why</u> do you think they wanted that?

Example: **To get their way.**

<u>Their</u> Truth and Needs

<u>Why</u> do you think they wanted that?

Example: **So they could put feet up.**

<u>Why</u> do you think they wanted that?

Example: **I guess so they could relax & be comfortable.**

What do you think the deepest part of this island is? What was their Positive Intention? Read page 28 for your reference. This is the deepest level of their destructive behavior and note that this is their **NEED →**

Really...

What did they ultimately want to FEEL?

Example: **PEACE** (To provide comfort to oneself is to feel peaceful)

Use this as a template to copy and reflect on future issues:

TIP OF THE ISLAND

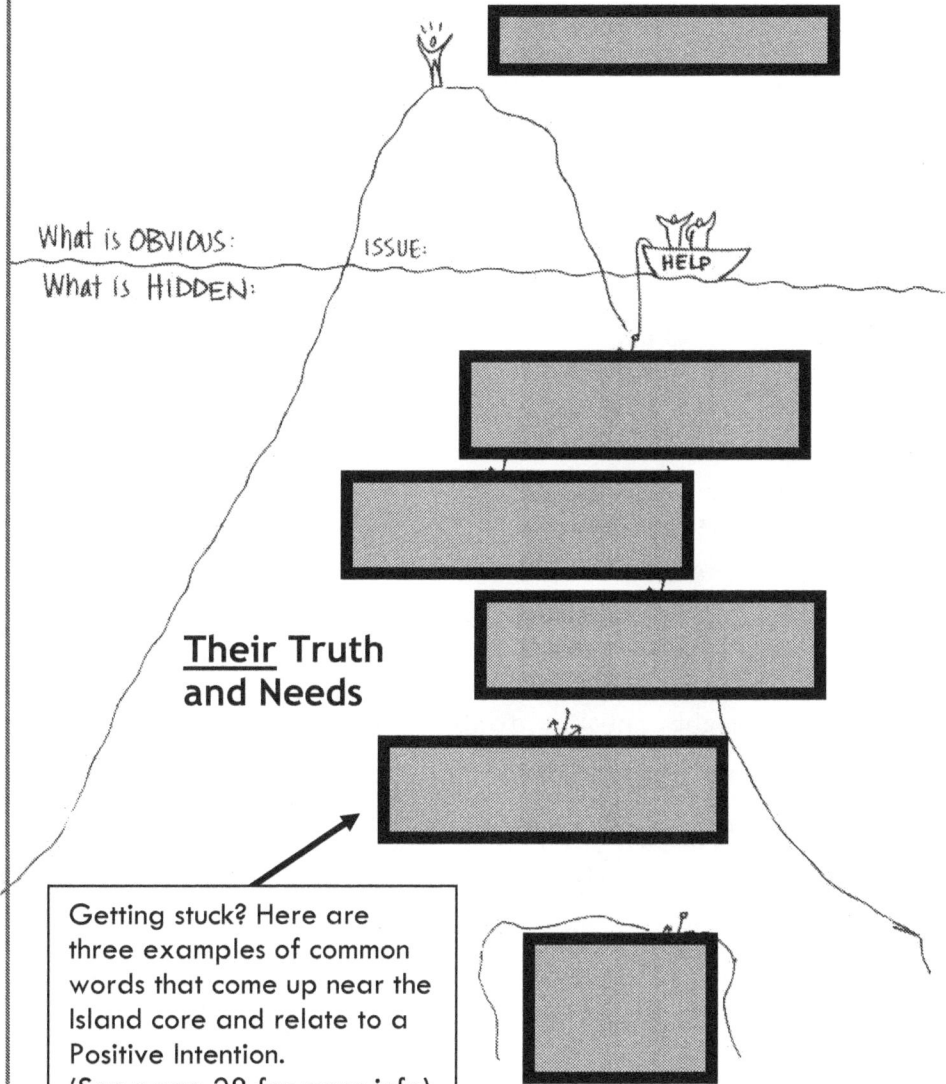

What is OBVIOUS:

What is HIDDEN:

ISSUE:

HELP

Their Truth and Needs

Getting stuck? Here are three examples of common words that come up near the Island core and relate to a Positive Intention.
(See page 28 for more info)
NEED FOR FUN = **LOVE**
NEED TO RELAX = **PEACE**
NEED FOR RESPECT = **LOVE**

Part Three: It's All About US!
My Way to [Our Way]

When I get upset, it is because someone broke my Rule and I feel like I already have "used" all of my positive behaviors (solutions) to get what I wanted. My positive solutions failed me, so I resort to destructive ones, including the solutions that relate to being upset (yelling, demanding, etc). My subconscious mind thinks, "These behaviors get more attention than my positive ones!" So I program my brain to actually **continue** resorting to negative solutions when my positive ones fail me, even though I only have Positive Intentions (See Activities 13&14, pg 33&34). Positive Intentions are just that – intentions. I intend to <u>feel</u> my Purpose. Even if I use a destructive temporary fix, I still get to feel it!

To break this ugly self-destructive cycle, I could become part of the solution rather than the problem. Instead of getting upset (a destructive solution that becomes their problem) or using any No! Rule, I could help the other person meet <u>their</u> Purpose by leading ON Purpose. Anything else is just insane. I might contribute to them by asking a **question** such as:

1) "What do you <u>need</u> right now?"
2) "What was your <u>intention</u> behind that?"
3) "Why did you <u>need</u> to do that?"

To find the positive intention of **any** destructive behavior, OUR WAY intends for both people to bring Activity 14 (pg 35) out in the open, rather than taking guesses. One asks question #3 above repeatedly and the other begins their answer with "Because I..." to uphold their responsibility.

36

Activity 15: Transforming Your Rule into a Contribution

Here, learn how to transform a Rule into a Contribution. For example, in Activity 6, both Yes! Rules were still set up to conflict. In OUR WAY, one person could have placed a blanket under their feet to get both of their needs met. Combining the Yes! Rules can lead to a contribution!

Think about how your Rule in Activity 4 (pg 18) set up room for someone to break it. How did you react? Did you use a _destructive_ solution (which became their problem)? What would have been a _constructive_ solution that could have contributed to their positive solution? Reflect on how this would have created an access for _them_ to express and experience _their_ Purpose.

If you could have **contributed** to the other person instead, what would that be? Write down your idea in the Left Circle. Your initial contribution could even be one of the 3 questions on page 36. This way, you find their positive intention (their need) and use this AS your contribution. For example, if someone disregards you, maybe they need Peace. Perhaps you could give them space & ask them about needs later.

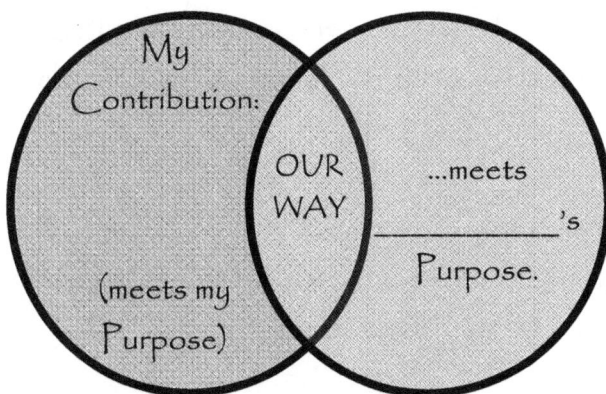

My
Contribution:

OUR
WAY   ...meets

_____'s

Purpose.

(meets my
Purpose)

In the Right Circle's blank, write the same person's name you wrote in Activity 4.

Final Remarks

If you have a difficult time expressing yourself constructively, these activities were designed to help you choose actions that lead into a desired future - without aggressive or passive-aggressive behavior.

You now can see that someone else's destructive behavior is like a cry out for living their Purpose, but they are stuck in a Rules-based life. You now have the tool to constructively express what you really want while contributing to the needs of another. You get to choose to make deposits rather than withdrawals into your relationship bank accounts!

The activities found in this book have promoted awareness, choice, and a life method for purposeful living. When you live on Purpose and seek OUR WAY over MY WAY, everything else follows.

The new context for your life is: Keep a clear connection to your Purpose, regardless of circumstances.

To start inventing this new life, choose to agree and complete the following **Action Plan**. After that, you might want to go back to Activity 2 (pg 16) and see if any of your "belief" answers turned from a NO to a YES. If not, explore what Rules might be holding you back from living on Purpose.

There is always a win-win situation waiting in infinite possibilities. Infinite possibilities begin when you genuinely ask "**What is it that you need?**" and you can create some sort of YES from there.

AGREEMENT & ACTION PLAN

Check far right box if you AGREE

OUR WAY™	ACTION PLAN	√
Activity 1: The Missing Word	I CHOOSE TO SEE THE DIFFERENCE BETWEEN WHAT A PERSON <u>IS</u> VERSUS WHAT A PERSON <u>IS BEING IN THE MOMENT</u>.	
Activity 2: My Current Thoughts & Behaviors	I CHOOSE TO TRANSFORM ANY ITEMS IN ACTIVITY 2's ASSESSMENT FROM A "NO" TO A "YES" THROUGHOUT MY LIFE. I WILL DO SO BY APPLYING THE LESSONS LEARNED IN THIS BOOK.	
Activity 3: My Rules	I CHOOSE TO BE AWARE THAT THE RULES I MAKE PROVIDE <u>ME</u> WAYS TO FEEL GOOD, BUT WHEN THEY CLASH WITH "THEIR" RULES, THEY DON'T.	
Activity 4: Broken Rules	I CHOOSE TO SEE HOW MY PROBLEMS ARE A RESULT OF MY OWN RULES. I CHOOSE TO NOT BLAME OTHERS FOR MY FEELINGS, THOUGHTS, AND ACTIONS BECAUSE I KNOW THEY STEM FROM MY OWN RULES.	
Activity 5: Advice, Requests, Habits	I CHOOSE TO SEE HOW MY <u>UNMET</u> REQUESTS, ADVICE, AND SUGGESTIONS ARE A RESULT OF ME NOT FULLY UNDERSTANDING "THEIR" NEEDS.	
Activity 6: No! Don't! Stop!	I CHOOSE TO TURN MY "NO! RULES" INTO "YES! RULES" SO THAT WE CAN BEGIN TO EXPLORE OUR WAY.	
Activity 7: My Solutions	I CHOOSE TO BE AWARE OF MY CHOSEN DESTRUCTIVE STRATEGIES AND UNDERSTAND HOW IT <u>DOES NOT</u> SERVE MY RELATIONSHIPS.	
Activity 8: My Islands	I CHOOSE TO BE AWARE OF MY DESTRUCTIVE SOLUTIONS.	

Activity 9: My Positive Intention	I CHOOSE TO GO ISLAND-DIVING TO FIND MY POSITIVE INTENTION.	
Activity 10: Who Am I?	I CHOOSE TO SEE MYSELF AS AN EVER-CHANGING ENTITY AND LOOK AT THE WORLD WITH THE NOTION OF "ANYTHING IS POSSIBLE."	
Activity 11: Is That Really Me?	I CHOOSE TO SEE THAT MY IDENTITY PORTRAYS <u>ASPECTS</u> OF ME - NOT MY TOTAL BEING.	
Activity 12: What Is My Purpose?	I CHOOSE TO LIVE & EXPRESS MY PURPOSE WHEN I SEE I'M DEMANDING IT FROM OTHERS TO FEEL IT. BY EXPRESSING IT, I WILL EXPERIENCE IT.	
Activity 13: Their Islands	I CHOOSE TO BE AWARE OF OTHER PEOPLE'S DESTRUCTIVE PATTERNS OF DEALING WITH THEIR BROKEN RULES.	
Activity 14: Their Positive Intention	I CHOOSE TO BE AWARE OF DESTRUCTIVE BEHAVIORS AS SIMPLY AN UNCONSCIOUS ATTEMPT TO FEEL PEACE, LOVE, SAFETY OR BELONGING.	
Activity 15: Transforming Rules into Contributions	I CHOOSE TO DO THE WORK TO TRANSFORM MY RULES INTO CONTRIBUTIONS AND EXPRESS THEM ON PURPOSE. I ALSO CHOOSE TO TAKE REQUESTS FOR <u>ME TO CHANGE</u> AS A GREAT OPPORTUNITY FOR ME TO CONTRIBUTE TO **THEIR** PURPOSE.	

Signature: _____

Date: _____

Glossary

- **Being:** How a person is existing in the moment. The way a person chooses to behave to get their needs met in the moment.
- **Expression:** How a person chooses to communicate their Purpose through words, symbols and/or body language.
- **Destructive Behavior:** A temporary fix to feel Purpose, usually done at the expense of another's Purpose.
- **Islands:** Destructive behaviors that people use to meet their needs.
- **MY WAY:** Rules a person invents and uses to momentarily experience their own Purpose, without interest for another's Purpose.
- **MY WAY to OUR WAY** ™: The transformation of Rules to Contributions.
- **Needs:** The ultimate reasons why a person does or says something.
- **On Purpose Living:** To contribute who we already are: being peaceful, safe, loving and without longing.
- **OUR WAY** ™: A contribution made on Purpose so another person can feel & express their Purpose as well.
- **Positive Intention:** The objective to FEEL peace, safety, belonging and love. People may resort to destructive behaviors to feel these.
- **Problem:** An unmet need.
- **Purpose:** In the **OUR WAY** ™ curriculum, it is to live & express four ultimate descriptives that define who we already ARE.
  - **Peace:** To BE without anxiety (or fear) of the past or future. In the truest of expression, it is positively serving the moment: <u>as it is</u> and not as it <u>should</u> or shouldn't be.
  - **Belonging:** To BE without longing. In the truest of expression, it is positively serving something larger than you, such as a relationship, group, or God.
  - **Safety:** To BE without danger. In the truest of expression, it is positively serving your own mental and physical state.
  - **Love:** To BE without fear. In the truest of expression, it is positively serving <u>your own</u> needs (peace, belonging and safety) so that the illusion of fear doesn't threaten your ability to contribute self-love or love to others (your Purpose).
- **Rule:** An expectation of <u>how</u> a person should express their Purpose.
- **Solution:** A chosen way of dealing with a conflict or a problem. Also referred to as "strategy"; "behavior"; or "island."
- **Transformation:** To see life (and the events that transpire) from a point of view that empowers the Self.

Island Index

ISLAND or DESTRUCTIVE SOLUTION	DEFINTION	EXAMPLE
1. *%$#!	To express vulgar language, usually with a louder, declarative voice.	*%$#!
2. Avoid	To not approach the person I have a problem with. OR To come up with a way to NOT think about the problem I have, regardless if my solution is negative or positive.	*[Staying clear of someone you don't want to talk to OR using some sort of escape as over-eating, drinking, smoking - or even yoga and dancing.*
3. Backstab	To express fault or weakness in someone. To devalue a person that is not present.	"She can be so mean!"
4. Belittle	To regard as small importance and brush aside.	"Well, that doesn't really matter..."
5. Blame	To put responsibility on someone else for my feelings, choice, or actions. To point the finger at another.	"She made me do it."
6. Brag	To talk proudly about what I own or what I can do to impress another.	"I have two of those!"
7. Centralize	To talk a lot about myself, my ideas and my experiences. To interrupt and relate to what others say to something about me.	"Oh! That reminds me of when I..."
8. Cheat	To act dishonestly to get what I want.	[Using any form of lying to get your way]
9. Compare	To notice a difference between two people, or things. For example, what is available and not available.	"If you were more like Jill, you'd be..."
10. Complain	To express what I don't want, usually to a safe person.	"I can't believe she would even do that!!"
11. Confuse	To create a state of misunderstanding, either as the communicator, or the receiver. To attempt to make someone confused in order to appear right. To give out mixed messages or appear ambiguous.	"Well, you said Saturday and then said Friday and I thought you meant next Friday!"

12. Control	To use power when no power is being experienced. To have power over what will be and how it will be.	*"I need you to do this. No questions asked."*
13. Criticize	To notice what doesn't meet my own standards and make the other person wrong for not meeting them.	*"If you knew how to dress, I might go out with you tonight."*
14. Correct	To infer my way of doing something as right and their way as wrong. The attempt to appear as intelligent.	*"Actually, the American Revolution wasn't in 1830..."*
15. Defend	To support my need in a competitive way. To blame someone else by denying their truth. To speak as if I was going to appear wrong, or not good enough. A preventative approach to losing.	*"Nooooo!! I was only trying to be..."*
16. Demand	To insist on what I want without regard for another's needs.	*"Come over here now!!"*
17. Deny	To say something is not true. To take the blame off of me.	*"It wasn't ME."*
18. Disregard	To agree to do something, but then choose NOT to do it. **OR** To <u>not</u> take notice in what someone is saying, but outwardly look agreeable.	*[Thinking, "What she is saying doesn't mean a thing to me..." as you nod.]*
19. Evaluate	To compare my expectation/ or ideal against what actually IS. To have a tendency to think my expressed opinion will become someone else's truth.	*"That's not good, John, not good at all."* **OR** *"You did great!"*
20. Exclude	To leave someone or a group of people out.	*"I'm sorry, but I really don't want him to be here."*
21. Fake	To pretend that something is true.	*"I'm fine, thanks."*
22. Fix	To come up with a quick solution to a long-term issue and not take into consideration all needs present.	*"Well, then I just won't talk then."*
23. Gossip	To talk about other person's business.	*"Oh, I saw her do THAT."*
24. Grumble	To make a deep gruff sound.	*"Ugh." [deep sighs]*
25. Hoard	To take more than is necessary.	*[You take the last one without asking]*

26. Humiliate	To hurt or attack someone's identity, often in front of people I want to impress.	*[You turn to your friends and laugh]* *"You look like a clown."*
27. Hunt	To consistently be on the search for confirming a fear I have.	*[Looking at someone's mail or diary]*
28. Ignore	To <u>not</u> appear as listening when being spoken to, but choosing to physically stay.	*[A person says something to you, but you say nothing at all while looking down]*
29. Insult	To use negative powerful words to attack identity of another.	*"You can be so ignorant. You can't even add."*
30. Interrogate	To incessantly ask questions to prove my prediction.	*"Where were you? What time did you call me? I didn't receive that call, did you call?"*
31. Interrupt	To talk over someone, without waiting to get my point across.	*"But! But I! I figured…"*
32. Invalidate	To cancel another person's actions or words, taking away any credit from them.	*"Now THAT'S a stupid idea."*
33. Jive	To only say part of what is expected.	*"No." "Yes."*
34. Joke	To make fun of someone - with a subtle truth hidden, unconscious or not. To point out something negative in humor while smiling. To apply sarcasm to hint my own opinion, usually using non-verbal communication, such as tone or gestures.	*"Oh, I was just kidding…"* **OR** *"Well, I thought YOU were perfect."*
35. Justify	To provide a reason for my feelings or behavior – usually basing reason on someone else's behavior.	*"I did that because…"*
36. Label	To attach a word to a behavior versus ultimately understanding another's expression.	*"What a weirdo."*
37. Mind-Read	To assume why someone did or said something and share it as truth. To not check-in with the other person's intentions.	*"Well you didn't call me 'cause you didn't want to!"*

38. Nag	To constantly ask for something or complain about something in a whiny tone, not considering someone else's reaction.	*"Oh go on! Let me have it, please? Please can I have it? I'll do what you want!!!"*
39. Name-call	To call someone a negative word.	*"Idiot."*
40. Personalize	To make meaning out of what another says or does as a confirmation of how I think.	*[Thinking, "She must have looked away because I said that."]*
41. Pout	To put out the bottom lip, or cross the arms with the head down.	
42. Punish	To make someone suffer for not meeting my own need via power over another.	*"Fine. I'm LEAVING."*
43. Resist	To fight back in an overt-aggressive (arguing) or passive-aggressive manner. Passive aggression is usually revealed through non-verbal behavior.	*"NOOOO!!"* OR *[You fold your arms silently]*
44. Score-keep	To keep score on what someone did or didn't do.	*"I did that LAST time!!"*
45. Shame	To express that a person didn't meet my need by embarrassing them.	*"WHY did you do THAT?? You must be ashamed of yourself."*
46. Shift	To change the subject to something not relevant to the conversation.	*"What ever happened to you doing what YOU said anyway?!"*
47. Should	To insist that my solution is the ideal answer to my problem.	*"You should act [this] way and shouldn't act [that] way."*
48. Smell	To pucker and snarl, pulling the top lip up and squint the eyes – for the purpose of revealing disgust in another.	
49. Snap	To make a quick comment in an attacking manner.	*"You don't listen to me – EVER!"*
50. Sorry	To say sorry in a negative tone, or to say it to avoid further shame.	*"Sorry- all RIGHT!"*

51. Sneer	To smile, squint the eyes, and perhaps shake the head.	
52. Steer	To answer a question with a question, to question the question, question the questioner, to change the subject.	*"Why do you even need to ask me that? Who gave you the right? That question has nothing to do with this."*
53. Tattle	To tell on someone and give the power to a third party to fix <u>my own</u> problem.	*"She did THAT to me!"*
54. Taunt	To try to get a negative reaction. To mock in a sarcastic, or insulting way.	*"Go on, <u>try</u> me."*
55. Tease	To make fun of someone, usually in front of person I want to impress.	*"Where did <u>you</u> come from?!" [laughing]*
56. Threaten	To pressure someone into doing it MY way by mentioning a future punishment if they don't abide.	*"If you don't do that, then I'll leave!"*
57. Walk Away	To physically withdraw from someone I am in communication with.	
58. Whine	To complain about something in a moaning, drawn-out, sad, or unpleasant way.	*"Pleeeeeease???"*
59. Withhold	To keep something hidden in order to avoid shame.	*[Thinking, "No way I'm gonna tell her THAT."]*
60. Yell	To raise my voice at someone in a stronger attempt to express my point.	*!!!*

Instead of applying the above destructive solutions to feel peace, safety, belonging or love, ask the other person:
"What do you need?" in a peaceful manner and see the relationship change before you...

Influential and Suggested Reading

The great Indian teacher Nisargadatta Maharaj once said:

"Wisdom tells me I am nothing. Love tells me I am everything.
Between the two my life flows."

Tao Te Ching, Lao Tzu	The 5 Love Languages, Gary Chapman
The Tao of Pooh, Benjamin Hoff	A Simpler Way, Meg Wheatley
Emotional Intelligence, Daniel Goleman	The Art of Possibility, Zander
Course of Miracles, Foundation for Inner Peace	Inspirational Sandwich, Sark
The Power of Now, Eckhart Tolle	The Power of Unconditional Love, Ken Keyes
The Significance of Life, Krishnamurti	Women Who Run With Wolves, Clarissa Pinkola Estes
Landmark Education	Neuro-Linguistic Programming ,(NLP) Richard Bandler
Six Thinking Hats, Edward DeBono	Love is Letting Go of Fear, Gerald G. Jampolsky

About the Author

The My Way to OUR WAY™
curriculum was developed, lived and
tested by a leadership expert, Jessie
Upp, with established experience in
fun and ENGAGING team play
facilitation, personal transformation,
and learning achievement.

Photo By: Karin Bigelow

Jessie Upp holds a Masters degree in Leadership with an emphasis in
Learning Development and a Bachelor's degree in Communications
focusing on Educational Technology.

Over the last 10 years, she has worked as an entrepreneurial multimedia
artist, corporate communication strategist, data analyst, technology
trainer, leadership coach, middle school elective teacher, and school
mediator. Her influences stem from a variety of learning and game
theories.

She resides in Edmonds, WA with her husband and 3 children.

Concrete life examples will soon be available in the
OUR WAY™ Booklet Series and website.

These resources provide familiar life scenarios that commonly
lead to upsets, conflict, and even anger.

Learn how to transform destructive behaviors
into constructive solutions today!

Growing Up OUR WAY
Engaged OUR WAY
Married OUR WAY
Parenting OUR WAY
Managing & Working OUR WAY

www.myway2ourway.com

www.ingramcontent.com/pod-product-compliance
Lightning Source LLC
Chambersburg PA
CBHW032036090426
42741CB00006B/834